The Texas Hill Country

A POSTCA.

GW00599521

PHOTOGRAPHS BY LAURENCE PARENT

These slightly oversized postcards require first-class postage

Laurence Parent Publishing
P.O. Box 849, Manchaca, Texas 78652

Printed by Best Printing, Austin, Texas

Designed by Kelleygraphics, Austin, Texas

Distributed by Falcon Press Publishing Co., Inc.
P.O. Box 1718, Helena, Montana 59624.
1-800-582-2665

Cover photo: Indian paintbrush, Texas bluebonnets, and phlox
surround the historic Danz cabin at Lyndon B. Johnson State and National
Historical Park. The cabin (now partly reconstructed) was built in the
mid-1800s by Casper Danz, one of the first German immigrants
to the Texas Hill Country.

About the photographer

Photographer and writer Laurence Parent has lived in the Austin area, at the edge of the Hill Country, for many years. Although his assignments take him all across the United States and to other countries, he sets aside time every year to photograph the Texas Hill Country. His work appears in many places, from state magazines such as *Texas Highways*, *Texas Monthly*, and *Texas Parks & Wildlife* to national publications such as *National Geographic Traveler*, Sierra Club Calendars, and Time-Life books.

☆ *Scattered ranches surround Enchanted Rock State Natural Area. The prominent granite dome lies in the heart of the Central Mineral Region of Texas.*

★ *Thousands of luminarias and electric lights brighten the River Walk at Christmas in San Antonio, Texas.*

☆ *Texas bluebonnets and phlox flourish in Central Texas, such as these just east of the Hill Country.*

☆ *A flaming sunset silhouettes the bell tower of Mission San Juan Capistrano. The mission, part of San Antonio Missions National Historical Park, Texas, was founded by the Spaniards in 1731*

☆ *The crystal-clear waters of the Pedernales River cascade over limestone ledges in Pedernales Falls State Park. The normally placid river is notorious for its sudden powerful floods.*

☆ *Indian blanket, horsemint (or lemon-mint), coreopsis, and clasping-leaved coneflower are among the multitudes of spring flowers found in the Texas Hill Country.*

☆ *Even today, windmills are a common method of providing water to homes and livestock on remote farms and ranches in the Texas Hill Country.*

☆ *A 45-foot waterfall cascades into Hamilton Pool, site of an old collapsed grotto. The pool, found in the Texas Hill Country west of Austin, is popular with swimmers in summer.*

☆ *The downtown skyline of Austin comes to life at dusk. Town Lake, a reservoir on the Colorado River, winds through the Texas capitol city.*

☆ *Ice from a rare winter storm frosts the fields and live oaks of the Texas Hill Country.*

☆ *Early Spanish settlers founded Mission Concepción of San Antonio Missions National Historical Park, Texas in 1731. The church's appearance has changed little in the many years since its construction.*

☆ *Maidenhair ferns thrive in the wet travertine deposited by spring-fed Gorman Falls. When the falls are opened to the public, they will be the highlight of the new Colorado Bend State Park, Texas*

☆ *In spring, Texas bluebonnets line the backroads of the Hill Country, such as this country lane in Gillespie County.*

☆ *Canned goods fill the pantry shelves of the Sauer-Beckmann Living History Farm at Lyndon B. Johnson State Historical Park, Texas. Through period work and dress, park employees at the farm depict life in the Hill Country in the early 1900s.*

☆ *Prickly pear cacti thrive in the rocky soils of the Texas Hill Country. People often harvest the fruits for use in jelly, syrup, and other foods.*

☆ *Basin sneezeweed and prickly pear maintain a toehold in the billion-year-old granite of Enchanted Rock State Natural Area, Texas.*

☆ *Fields of Texas bluebonnets and Indian paintbrush display their colors throughout the Hill Country and Central Texas every spring.*

☆ *Bigtooth maples survive in the headwaters of the Sabinal River in Lost Maples State Natural Area, Texas. Deep canyons protect the trees from drying winds and high summer temperatures.*

☆ *The granite dome of Enchanted Rock is reflected in the still waters of Moss Lake in Enchanted Rock State Natural Area, Texas. The dome is but a small part of the igneous feature known as the Enchanted Rock batholith.*

☆ *In fall, the bigtooth maples of Lost Maples State Natural Area turn scarlet and gold. The maples produce the best autumn color in the Texas Hill Country.*

☆ *Bald cypresses line Cibolo Creek near Boerne, Texas.*
Cypresses thrive in the extra moisture found along permanent
streams and rivers in the Hill Country.

☆ *The prominent University of Texas tower is visible from the fountain at the Lyndon B. Johnson Library in Austin. The library houses the museum and archives chronicling Johnson's presidency.*